~≈ Presented to

~≈ On the occasion of

~≈ With prayers and best wishes from

PRAYERS FOR Young CATHOLICS

Compiled by
the Daughters of St. Paul

Pauline
BOOKS & MEDIA
Boston

Nihil Obstat:
  Fr. Mariusz Beczek, OSJ, STD

Imprimatur:
  ✝ José H. Gomez, STD
  Archbishop of Los Angeles
  June 7, 2013

Library of Congress Cataloging-in-Publication Data

Prayers for young Catholics / compiled by the Daughters of St. Paul.
    pages cm
  ISBN 978-0-8198-5995-2 -- ISBN 0-8198-5995-8
  1. Catholic Church--Prayers and devotions--Juvenile literature. 2. Catholic
children--Prayers and devotions. I. Daughters of St. Paul.
  BX2150.P73 2014
  242'.82--dc23

                                            2013045619

First edition copyright © 2014, Daughters of St. Paul

Published by Pauline Books & Media, 50 Saint Pauls Avenue, Boston, MA 02130-3491

Printed in Korea

PFYC SIPSKOGUNKYO1-14047 5995-8

www.pauline.org

Pauline Books & Media is the publishing house of the Daughters of St. Paul, an international
congregation of women religious serving the Church with the communications media.

2 3 4 5 6 7 8 9   20 19 18 17 16

❧ CONTENTS

I. Basic Prayers

II. Prayers to Mary

III. Prayers to the Saints

IV. Prayers from the Bible

V. Prayers for Various Needs

BASIC
PRAYERS

Prayer is a conversation with God. In every relationship and friendship, communication or talking is necessary for that relationship to continue to grow and be strong. This is true if your relationship or friendship is with a family member, your best friend, or God.

Your conversations with God can take many forms: you can sing; you can pray the prayers in this book; or you can talk to God using your own words. The important thing is to keep your friendship with God healthy by talking to him every day.

The Sign of the Cross

In the name
of the Father,

and of the Son,

and of the Holy

Spirit.

Amen.

5

Morning Offering

O Jesus, through the Immaculate Heart of Mary, I offer you my prayers, works, joys, and sufferings of this day, for all the intentions of your Sacred Heart, in union with the Holy Sacrifice of the Mass throughout the world, in reparation for my sins, for the intentions of all my relatives and friends, and in particular for the intentions of the Holy Father. Amen.

The Lord's Prayer

Our Father, who art in heaven, hallowed be thy name. Thy kingdom come, Thy will be done on earth as it is in heaven. Give us this day our daily bread, and forgive us our trespasses, as we forgive those who trespass against us. And lead us not into temptation, but deliver us from evil. Amen.

Hail Mary

Hail Mary, full of grace, the Lord is with you. Blessed are you among women, and blessed is the fruit of your womb, Jesus. Holy Mary, Mother of God, pray for us sinners, now and at the hour of our death. Amen.

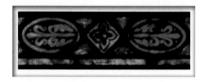

Glory

Glory
to the Father,
and to the Son,
and to the Holy Spirit:
as it was in the beginning, is now,
and will be for ever. Amen.

The Apostles' Creed

I believe in God, the Father
    almighty,
Creator of heaven and earth,

and in Jesus Christ, his only Son,
 our Lord,
(Here we bow until after the words "the Virgin Mary.")
who was conceived by the Holy
 Spirit,
born of the Virgin Mary,
suffered under Pontius Pilate,
was crucified, died and was buried;
he descended into hell;
on the third day he rose again from
 the dead;
he ascended into heaven,
and is seated at the right hand of God
 the Father almighty;
from there he will come to judge the
 living and the dead.
I believe in the Holy Spirit,
the holy catholic Church,
the communion of saints,
the forgiveness of sins,
the resurrection of the body,
and life everlasting. Amen.

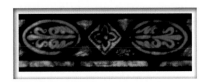

Act of Faith

O my God, I firmly believe that you are one God in three Divine Persons, Father, Son, and Holy Spirit; I believe that your Divine Son became man and died for our sins, and that he will come again to judge the living and the dead. I believe these and all the truths which the holy Catholic Church teaches, because you have revealed them who can neither deceive nor be deceived.

Act of Hope

O my God, relying on your infinite goodness and promises, I hope to obtain pardon of my sins, the help of your grace, and life everlasting, through the merits of Jesus Christ, my Lord and Redeemer.

Act of Love

O my God, I love you above all things, with my whole heart and soul, because you are all good and worthy of all love. I love my neighbor as myself for the love of you. I forgive all who have injured me and ask pardon of all whom I have injured.

Act of Contrition

My God,
I am sorry for my sins with all my heart.
In choosing to do wrong
and failing to do good,
I have sinned against you
whom I should love above all things.
I firmly intend, with your help,
to do penance,
to sin no more,
and to avoid whatever leads me to sin.
Our Savior Jesus Christ
suffered and died for us.
In his name, my God, have mercy.

Prayer Before a Crucifix

Look down upon me, good and gentle Jesus, while I kneel before you. I ask you to give me faith, hope, and love, true sorrow for my sins, and the desire to please you more and more. I look with great love and sorrow at your five wounds. And I remember the words which David your prophet said of you, my Jesus: "They have pierced my hands and my feet; they have counted all my bones."

Prayer to the Holy Spirit

Come, Holy Spirit, fill the hearts
of your faithful people. Make the fire of
your love burn in us. Come and make
all creation new.

Prayer for Those Who Have Died

Eternal rest grant unto them,
    O Lord,
and let perpetual light shine upon
    them.
May they rest in peace. Amen.

Prayer to My
Guardian Angel

Angel of God, my guardian dear, to whom God's love entrusts me here. Ever this day be at my side, to light and guard, to rule and guide. Amen.

Prayer Before Meals

Bless us, O Lord, and these your gifts which we are about to receive from your bounty, through Christ our Lord. Amen.

Prayer After Meals

We give you thanks for all your benefits, O loving God, you who live and reign forever. Amen.

Prayer at Night

I adore you, my God, and I love you with all my heart. I thank you for having created me, made me a Christian, and kept me this day. Thank you for the good things I have done today. Forgive me all my sins. Take care of me while I sleep and deliver me from all danger. May your grace be always with me and with all my loved ones. Amen.

PRAYERS TO MARY

Jesus gives us himself, but he also gives us his mother, Mary. Mary is not God, but because she was chosen to be the Mother of God's Son, she has a special place in his heart. When we pray to Mary, we are asking her to pray with us and intercede for us. She did this for the bride and groom at the wedding in Cana, where Jesus performed his first miracle and changed water into wine. As our heavenly Mother, Mary loves us, helps us, and leads us to a deeper relationship with Jesus.

The Angelus

V. The angel spoke God's message to Mary,
R. and she conceived of the Holy Spirit.

Hail Mary . . .

V. "I am the lowly servant of the Lord:
R. "Let it be done to me according to your
word."

Hail Mary . . .

V. And the Word became flesh
R. and lived among us.

Hail Mary . . .

V. Pray for us, holy Mother of God,
R. that we may become worthy of the
promises of Christ.

Let us pray.

Lord,
fill our hearts with your grace:
once, through the message of an angel
you revealed to us the incarnation of your
Son;
now through his suffering and death
lead us to the glory of his resurrection.
We ask this through Christ our Lord.
Amen.

Regina Coeli

V. Queen of Heaven, rejoice, alleluia.
R. The Son whom you were
    privileged to bear, alleluia.

V. Has risen as he said, alleluia.
R. Pray to God for us, alleluia.

V. Rejoice and be glad, Virgin Mary,
    alleluia.
R. For the Lord has truly risen,
    alleluia.

Let us pray.

O God, it was by the Resurrection of
your Son, our Lord Jesus Christ, that
you brought joy to the world. Grant that
through the intercession of the Virgin
Mary, his Mother, we may attain the joy
of eternal life. Through Christ, our Lord.
Amen.

Magnificat

See Luke 1:46-55

My soul proclaims the greatness of the
    Lord,
my spirit rejoices in God my Savior;
for he has looked with favor on his
    lowly servant.
From this day all generations will call
    me blessed:
the Almighty has done great things for
    me,
and holy is his Name.
He has mercy on those who fear him
in every generation.
He has shown the strength of his arm,
he has scattered the proud in their
    conceit.
He has cast down the mighty from their
    thrones,
and has lifted up the lowly.
He has filled the hungry with good
    things,
and the rich he has sent away empty.

He has come to the help of his servant
  Israel
for he has remembered his promise of
  mercy,
the promise he made to our fathers,
to Abraham and his children for ever.

Hail, Holy Queen

Hail, holy Queen, Mother of Mercy, our life, our sweetness, and our hope. To you do we cry, poor banished children of Eve; to you do we send up our sighs, mourning and weeping in this valley of tears. Turn then, most gracious advocate, your eyes of mercy toward us, and after this our exile, show unto us the blessed fruit of your womb, Jesus. O clement, O loving, O sweet Virgin Mary.

Dear and Sweet Mother Mary

Dear and sweet Mother Mary,
keep your holy hand upon me; guard my
mind, my heart, and my senses, that I may
never commit sin. Sanctify my thoughts,
affections, words, and actions, so that I may
please you and your Jesus, my God, and
reach heaven with you. Jesus and Mary,
give me your holy blessing: In the name of
the Father, and of the Son, and of the Holy
Spirit *(make the Sign of the Cross)*. Amen.

Memorare

Remember, O most gracious Virgin
Mary, that never was it known that anyone
who fled to your protection, implored your
help, or sought your intercession, was left
unaided. Inspired with this confidence,
I fly to you, O Virgin of virgins, my mother;
to you do I come, before you I stand, sinful
and sorrowful. O Mother of the Word
Incarnate, despise not my petitions, but in
your mercy hear and answer me. Amen.

Litany of Loreto

Lord, have mercy on us.

Christ, have mercy on us

Lord, have mercy on us.

God the Father of Heaven,
have mercy on us,

God the Son, Redeemer of the world,
have mercy on us,

God the Holy Spirit, have mercy on us,

Holy Trinity, One God,
have mercy on us,

Holy Mary, pray for us.

("Pray for us" is repeated after each invocation.)

Holy Mother of God,

Holy Virgin of virgins,

Mother of Christ,

Mother of Divine Grace,

Mother most pure,

Mother most chaste,

Mother inviolate,

Mother undefiled,

Mother most amiable,

Mother most admirable,
Mother of good counsel,
Mother of our Creator,
Mother of our Savior,
Mother of the Church,
Virgin most prudent,
Virgin most venerable,
Virgin most renowned,
Virgin most powerful,
Virgin most merciful,
Virgin most faithful,

Mirror of justice,
Seat of wisdom,
Cause of our joy,
Spiritual vessel,
Vessel of honor,
Singular vessel of devotion,
Mystical rose,
Tower of David,
Tower of ivory,
House of gold,
Ark of the covenant,
Gate of Heaven,
Morning star,
Health of the sick,
Refuge of sinners,
Comforter of the afflicted,
Help of Christians,
Queen of patriarchs and prophets,
Queen of apostles and martyrs,
Queen of confessors and virgins,
Queen of angels and saints,

Queen conceived without original sin,
Queen assumed into Heaven,
Queen of the holy Rosary,
Queen of families,
Queen of peace,

Lamb of God, who takes away the sins of
the world, spare us, O Lord.
Lamb of God, who takes away the sins of
the world, graciously spare us, O Lord.
Lamb of God, who takes away the sins of
the world, have mercy on us.
Pray for us, O holy Mother of God,
that we may be made worthy
of the promises of Christ.

O God, whose only-begotten Son, by his
life, death, and resurrection, has purchased
for us the rewards of eternal life, grant,
we beseech you, that by meditating upon
these mysteries of the most holy Rosary of
the Blessed Virgin Mary, we may imitate
what they contain, and obtain what they
promise. Through Christ our Lord. Amen.

PRAYERS TO THE SAINTS

The saints are Catholics who lived holy lives and show us virtues to a heroic degree.

The Church recognizes saints in order to give us good examples of how to live our faith in Jesus. The saints help us with their prayers. We pray to the saints to ask them to pray to God for us and also with us. Oftentimes we associate saints with a specific place, interest, or need. When we do this, we say that the saint is a patron saint.

Prayer to Saint Joseph

Saint Joseph, God chose you to be the foster father of Jesus here on earth. Please ask Jesus to bless my father and all the fathers in the world. Remember, too, our Holy Father, the Pope. Saint Joseph, you are also the patron of the universal Church. Watch over the Catholic Church in a special way, so that all the members of our Church will grow closer and closer to Jesus, and teach many other people about him too. Amen.

Prayer to Saint Thérèse of Lisieux

Saint Thérèse, you found a way to do even the smallest actions out of love for God. Teach me little ways to love God and other people. Show me that everything done with love is important. I want to love Jesus and Mary very much, as you did. Amen.

Prayer to Saint Paul

Saint Paul, once Jesus revealed himself to you as God's Son, you spent your whole life loving him and teaching others about him. This made you an apostle and missionary. Inspire me to be an apostle and missionary of Jesus, too. Help me to spread the good news of Jesus to everyone I meet. Let my words and actions always show that I am a follower of Jesus. Amen.

Prayer to Saint Michael the Archangel

Saint Michael the Archangel, defend us in battle. Be our protection against the wickedness and snares of the devil. May God rebuke him, we humbly pray; and may you, O Prince of the heavenly host, by the power of God cast into hell Satan and all the evil spirits who prowl about the world seeking the ruin of souls. Amen.

Prayer to Saint Gabriel the Archangel

Saint Gabriel, you were sent to the Virgin Mary to tell her that God had chosen her to be the Mother of his Son. You are the special protector of all people who send messages: postal workers, delivery people, radio and television workers and broadcasters, and all those who work in communications. Help these people to speak of God's love and faithfulness. When I communicate in any way, help me to be a messenger of God's love as you are. Amen.

Prayer to Saint Raphael the Archangel

Saint Raphael, you are the patron saint of travelers and of people who are sick. Your mission is to bring people health and safety. Please pray for all people traveling today. Guide them and help them to travel in safety and in peace. Please also pray for those who are suffering with illnesses. Give them peace, patience, and healing. Amen.

Prayer to Saint Faustina

Saint Faustina, you were privileged to receive many messages from Jesus while you lived here on earth. Jesus taught you to trust in him completely, and asked you to spread a devotion to his divine mercy among all believers. Pray for me so that I may accept the forgiveness and mercy Jesus so lovingly offers and that I may also be an instrument of his mercy in our world. Amen.

Prayer to Saint John Bosco

Saint John Bosco, you helped many students during your life on earth, and now in heaven you continue to pray in a special way for all students. God's call for me now is to be a student. Help me to study hard and do my very best in school. Pray that what I study may lead me to a deeper understanding of God, his creation, his love, and his plan for me. Amen.

Prayer to Saint Marguerite Bourgeoys

Saint Marguerite, when you were a young woman, you courageously emigrated from France to Canada. You left your home in order to teach and take care of poor uneducated children. As most good teachers do, you put your students' needs ahead of your own. Please join me in praying for my teachers that they may also be witnesses to God's love and care in the lives of their students. Amen.

Prayer to Saint Elizabeth Ann Seton

Saint Elizabeth Ann Seton, you loved children and started the first Catholic schools in the United States in order to help them learn and strengthen their faith. Now you are a patron of Catholic schools. I place myself and my studies under your protection. Pray for me, that I may grow closer to Jesus through all that I learn. Amen.

Prayer to Saint Martin de Porres

Saint Martin, you cared for children by founding a children's hospital and orphanage in Peru. Now you are a patron saint of public schools. I ask you to pray for me and my studies, so that I may grow closer to Jesus with each day of learning. Amen.

Prayer to Saint Catherine of Bologna

Saint Catherine, as an artist and painter you proclaimed the beauty of all God's creation. Pray for all artists, that with their gifts they may help all people see the beauty of our world. Help me, also, to appreciate the gift of art and the many ways that it can be used to glorify God. Amen.

Prayer to Saint Sebastian

Saint Sebastian, you were a soldier who witnessed to your faith in Jesus by giving your life for him. Now you are the patron of athletes and their special protector. Help me to thank God for the ability to play sports whether I win or lose. Pray for me that I may be safe when I play, and help me to glorify God by doing my best. Amen.

Prayer to Saint Cecilia

Saint Cecilia, I pray to you in a special way for musicians. Music is an amazing way to praise God. Help me to thank God for the gift of music and for my ability to make music by singing or playing instruments. Every time I sing, play, or listen to music, I ask you to remind me of God's goodness and love. Amen.

Prayer to Saint Genesius

Saint Genesius, you were an actor who converted to Christianity during a play on the stage. Help me to thank God for the gift of drama. Please pray that God will be glorified by all actors and those who work in the theater, television, and movies. Pray for me, too, when I am involved in acting or in the theater. Help me to be a witness to the greatest truth of all—God's love for us. Amen.

Prayer to Saint Clare

Saint Clare, you are the patron saint of television. Join me in praying for all those that work as actors, writers, directors, and all those who work on television programs. Help them to use their talents to produce programs that give people hope and encourage respect for others. Pray for me that I may choose wisely what I watch on television. Amen.

Prayer to Saint Kateri Tekakwitha

Saint Kateri, when you were young, you were often bullied by some of the members of your tribe. Today, many children are bullied like you were. Help me to stand up for myself and others, to be a kind and caring friend to all. Join me in praying for bullies, too, that they may come to realize that what they are doing is hurtful. May they receive the grace to respect the dignity of all people. Amen.

PRAYERS
FROM THE
BIBLE

The Bible is God's Word. It also contains many prayers. In this section, you will find a small selection of the prayers found in the Bible.

Prayer of God's Love

Ephesians 3:17–21

[May Christ] dwell in your hearts through faith, as you are being rooted and grounded in love. I pray that you may have the power to comprehend, with all the saints, what is the breadth and length and height and depth, and to know the love of Christ that surpasses knowledge, so that you may be filled with all the fullness of God.

Now to him who by the power at work within us is able to accomplish abundantly far more than all we can ask or imagine, to him be glory in the church and in Christ Jesus to all generations, forever and ever. Amen.

Prayer of Praise

Psalm 150

Praise the LORD!
Praise God in his sanctuary; praise him
    in his mighty firmament!
Praise him for his mighty deeds; praise
    him according to his surpassing
      greatness!
Praise him with trumpet sound; praise
    him with lute and harp!
Praise him with tambourine and dance;
    praise him with strings and pipe!
Praise him with clanging cymbals;
    praise him with loud clashing cymbals!
Let everything that breathes praise the
    LORD!
Praise the LORD!

Prayer for Guidance

Ephesians 1:3–4, 8–10

Blessed be the God and Father of our Lord Jesus Christ, who has blessed us in Christ with every spiritual blessing in the heavenly places, just as he chose us in Christ before the foundation of the world to be holy and blameless before him in love.

With all wisdom and insight he has made known to us the mystery of his will, according to his good pleasure that he set forth in Christ, as a plan for the fullness of time, to gather up all things in him, things in heaven and things on earth.

Prayer of Trust

Psalm 27:1–4

The LORD is my light and my
    salvation; whom shall I fear?
The LORD is the stronghold of my life;
    of whom shall I be afraid?
When evildoers assail me to devour my
    flesh—
my adversaries and foes—they shall
    stumble and fall.
Though an army encamp against me,
    my heart shall not fear;
though war rise up against me, yet I will
    be confident.
One thing I asked of the LORD, that
    will I seek after:
to live in the house of the LORD all
    the days of my life,
to behold the beauty of the LORD, and
to inquire in his temple.

Prayer to Lead a Good Life

Deuteronomy 6:4–9

Hear, O Israel: The LORD is our God, the LORD alone. You shall love the LORD your God with all your heart, and with all your soul, and with all your might. Keep these words that I am commanding you today in your heart. Recite them to your children and talk about them when you are at home and when you are away, when you lie down and when you rise. Bind them as a sign on your hand, fix them as an emblem on your forehead, and write them on the doorposts of your house and on your gates.

Prayer to Love Others

1 Corinthians 13:4–8

Love is patient; love is kind; love is not envious or boastful or arrogant or rude. It does not insist on its own way; it is not irritable or resentful; it does not rejoice in wrongdoing, but rejoices in the truth. It bears all things, believes all things, hopes all things, endures all things. Love never ends.

In Praise of the Divine Shepherd

Psalm 23

The LORD is my shepherd, I shall not
     want. He makes me lie down in
     green pastures;
he leads me beside still waters;
     he restores my soul.
He leads me in right paths for his
     name's sake.
Even though I walk through the darkest
     valley, I fear no evil;
for you are with me; your rod and your
staff—they comfort me.
You prepare a table before me in the
     presence of my enemies;
you anoint my head with oil; my cup
     overflows.
Surely goodness and mercy shall follow
me all the days of my life,
and I shall dwell in the house of the
     LORD my whole life long.

71

Prayer of Thanksgiving

Luke 1:68–79

Blessed be the Lord God of Israel, for
    he has looked favorably on his people
    and redeemed them.
He has raised up a mighty savior for us
    in the house of his servant David,
as he spoke through the mouth of his
    holy prophets from of old, that we
    would be saved from our enemies and
    from the hand of all who hate us.
Thus he has shown the mercy promised
    to our ancestors, and has remembered
    his holy covenant,
the oath that he swore to our ancestor
    Abraham, to grant us that we, being
    rescued from the hands of our enemies,

might serve him without fear,
    in holiness and righteousness before
    him all our days.
And you, child, will be called the
    prophet of the Most High; for you will
    go before the Lord to prepare his ways,
to give knowledge of salvation to his people
    by the forgiveness of their sins.
By the tender mercy of our God, the
    dawn from on high will break upon us,
to give light to those who sit in darkness
    and in the shadow of death, to guide
    our feet into the way of peace.

PRAYERS
FOR VARIOUS
NEEDS

Intercessory prayer is when we pray asking God for a particular need that others may have. As members of the Body of Christ, we can and should pray for one another.

For My Family

Jesus, while on earth you belonged
to a family. You lived with your mother,
Mary, and your foster father, Saint Joseph.
Together, you formed the Holy Family.
I am part of a family, too. Jesus, watch
over my family. Protect us and keep us
safe. Bless us and bring us all closer to you.
Amen.

For My Dad

O God, you are my heavenly Father,
and you take care of me. You gave me my
dad to help take care of me on earth. Bless
my dad. Help him to make wise and loving
decisions. Forgive him for the times he falls
short. Take care of him, strengthen him,
and bring him close to you. Amen.

For My Mom

Jesus, when you were young you truly loved your mother, Mary. When you were on the cross, you gave her to all of us as our mother, too. You have also given me my mom. I ask you to bless my mom and take care of her. Please give her all the grace she needs to do your will. Forgive her when she loses patience or becomes discouraged. Show me by your example how to love and obey my mom. Amen.

For My Siblings

Lord God, thank you for the brothers and sisters you gave me. They are very special to me. Even though sometimes we don't get along, I always love them. Forgive me for the times I haven't shown them my love. Bless each of them and give them the special graces they need to become what you created them to be. Help me to love them as you do. Amen.

For My Friends

Jesus, you gave me the gift of my friends. Their friendship and love remind me of your love and faithfulness. Thank you for my friends. Help me to be a good friend to each of them. Teach me to be someone who listens, serves, and loves. Let all of my friendships be modeled on my relationship with you. Help me always to remember that you are my best friend. Amen.

For All Children

Jesus, you said, "Let the little children come to me." I pray for all children of the world: for those in my school, in my town, in my country, but also for those in all schools, towns, and countries of the world. Protect us from all harm and danger. Help us to study well in school, to love our families and friends, to respect one another, and to play fairly and safely. Help us to come closer to you every day, and to act like children of God the Father. Amen.

For the Church

Heavenly Father, I pray for the Catholic Church: for the pope, for the bishops, for all priests and deacons, religious brothers and sisters, pastoral ministers, catechists, and for all Catholics. I pray especially for the bishop of my diocese; for the pastor, priests, and deacons of my parish; for any religious sisters or brothers at my parish or school; for those who lead or teach; and for all the Catholics in my parish and neighborhood. Help us to be faithful to you and to be compassionate toward one another. Amen.

For Those Who Are Sick

Dear Jesus, many people in the world are sick and suffering right now. Some of them are seriously ill, others less seriously, and still others are anxiously waiting for results of medical tests. You know each of them; you understand their fears, and you hold them in your heart. Bless the people I know who are sick *(you may wish to name them)*. Bless everyone who is suffering. May they feel how close you are to them. And if it is your will, Lord, heal them. Amen.

For Those Who Have Died

Dear God, we know that our life here on earth is passing. Give all people who have died eternal rest, light, and peace with you. I pray especially for *(you may wish to name people you know who have died)*. Give those who loved them peace, hope, and consolation. Help us all to trust in your care for us, in this life and in the next. Amen.

For Peace

God of peace, there are many places in the world where there is conflict and war, many situations in which it is difficult to find peace. People are afraid, hurt, and suffering. But Jesus came to bring us peace and love. I pray for peace in the world, especially the parts of the world where there is tension and war. Show all people how to listen to one another, accept differences, and live in peace with one another, for you are the Father of all. Amen.

For Those Who Do Not Yet Know God

Dear Jesus, you came to earth so that all people could know you, the Father, and the Holy Spirit. You wanted to show everyone how much you love them. Thank you for the gift of faith that you have given me through my family and the Church. There are people today who do not know you, and others who have turned away from you. I offer you my prayers and sacrifices today so that these people will come to experience you and your love. Help me to make you known by what I say and the way I live. Amen.

To Know and Answer God's Call for Me

Holy Spirit, you have a special call—
a special vocation—for my life. I do not
know yet what it is or what I will become.
But I want to live with you at the center
of my life. I believe that you will show me
your will for me. Help me to be open to
your call, and give me the grace to answer
it. Amen.

THE
ROSARY

How to Pray the Rosary

We pray the Rosary to honor Jesus and his mother, Mary. When we pray, we can use a set of beads. We say a prayer as we touch each bead. As we pray, we think about some important times in the lives of Jesus and Mary. These important times are called the mysteries of the Rosary. Thinking about these times helps us to come closer to Jesus by remembering his life. The Rosary also helps us to tell Jesus about our lives.

4. Pray the Glory (page 9)
Name the 1st mystery
Pray the Lord's Prayer

5. Pray 10 Hail Marys

14. Pray the Glory
and the Hail,
Holy Queen (page 30)

3. Pray 3
Hail Marys
(page 9)

15. Kiss the crucifix

2. Pray the Lord's Prayer
(page 8)

1. Make the
Sign of the Cross (page 5)
and pray the Apostles'
Creed (page 10)

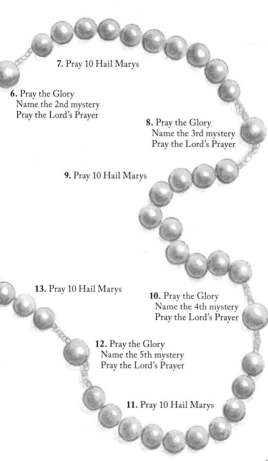

7. Pray 10 Hail Marys

6. Pray the Glory
   Name the 2nd mystery
   Pray the Lord's Prayer

8. Pray the Glory
   Name the 3rd mystery
   Pray the Lord's Prayer

9. Pray 10 Hail Marys

13. Pray 10 Hail Marys

10. Pray the Glory
   Name the 4th mystery
   Pray the Lord's Prayer

12. Pray the Glory
   Name the 5th mystery
   Pray the Lord's Prayer

11. Pray 10 Hail Marys

The Joyful Mysteries

*We pray
the joyful mysteries on
Mondays and Saturdays.*

The Annunciation
of the Archangel Gabriel to Mary

Through the Archangel Gabriel,
God asked Mary to be the Mother
of his Son, Jesus. Mary, help me
to say "yes" to God as you did.

The Visitation of Mary to Her Cousin Elizabeth

Mary visited her cousin Elizabeth to bring her good news and to help her. Mary, teach me how to share good news and help others too.

The Nativity

Jesus was born in a stable in the small town of Bethlehem. Jesus, thank you for being born for us, to show us how to live!

The Presentation in the Temple

Mary and Joseph presented Jesus to God in the Temple. Jesus, help me to offer each day to God just as you were offered.

The Finding of Jesus in the Temple

Mary and Joseph found Jesus speaking with the priests and teachers in the Temple about God his Father. Jesus, help me to obey God and my parents in the same way you did.

The Mysteries of Light

*We pray
the mysteries of light
on Thursdays.*

The Baptism of Jesus

John the Baptist baptized Jesus in the Jordan River. Jesus, thank you for being baptized to show us how to begin our life in you.

The Wedding at Cana

Jesus did as Mary asked and worked his first miracle at the wedding at Cana by turning water into wine. Mary, help me to trust in your Son.

Jesus Announces God's Kingdom

Jesus spent three years teaching people about God's love and telling them to return to God. Jesus, show me how I can announce God's kingdom to the people in my life.

The Transfiguration

Jesus took Peter, James, and John up a mountain and began to shine with God's glory. Jesus, help me to see you in each person I meet today.

Jesus Gives Us the Holy Eucharist

At the Last Supper, Jesus changed bread and wine into his Body and Blood. Jesus, thank you for this gift—I want to receive you in Holy Communion often!

The Sorrowful Mysteries

*We pray
the sorrowful mysteries
on Tuesdays and Fridays.*

The Agony in the Garden

Jesus prayed to be able to accept what God his Father asked him to do. Jesus, I pray for those who are struggling to accept God's will for them.

The Scourging at the Pillar

Jesus was whipped by the soldiers and suffered very much. Jesus, I pray that those who are suffering today may feel you close to them.

The Crowning with Thorns

The soldiers made fun of Jesus by putting a crown of thorns on him and pretending to honor him. Jesus, help me not to make fun of others but to say and do positive things.

The Carrying of the Cross

Jesus carried his own heavy cross to the place where he would die. Jesus, forgive me for the times I did not listen to you and sinned.

The Crucifixion

Jesus was nailed to the cross and died for us, and Mary was there watching and suffering with him. Mary, help me to remember how much Jesus loves me. Pray for me that I may love Jesus more each day.

The Glorious Mysteries

*We pray
the glorious mysteries
on Wednesdays
and Sundays.*

The Resurrection

On Easter Sunday morning, Jesus rose from the dead! Jesus, thank you for the new life that your resurrection gives us.

The Ascension

Jesus returned to
heaven to be with
God his Father.
Jesus, help me to
tell everyone about
you and your love,
as you told your disciples to do.

The Descent of
the Holy Spirit

The Holy Spirit
came down on
Mary and the
disciples. Mary, ask
the Holy Spirit to
come down on me and make my faith,
hope, and love grow.

The Assumption

Mary was taken body and soul into heaven, where she is now with Jesus. Mary, pray for me and help me make decisions that will lead me to heaven, too.

The Coronation

Mary is the Queen of heaven and earth. Mary, you are my Queen too, and I trust you to bring me always closer to Jesus.

THE STATIONS OF THE CROSS

We pray the Stations of the Cross to remember how and why Jesus died for us. We pray them especially on Fridays and during the season of Lent, the time of preparation for Easter. Each station recalls something that happened to Jesus from the time he left the Last Supper through the events of Good Friday. Sometimes we pray them in church, where we can look at pictures of each of the stations. Thinking about the stations helps us remember how much Jesus loves us.

How to Pray
the Stations of the Cross

If you are with a group, the leader may announce the station and say, "We adore you, O Christ, and we bless you." The group may respond, "Because by your holy cross you have redeemed the world." A reader may proclaim the Scripture reading, and the group may respond with the prayer.

Opening Prayer

Dear Jesus, who died to save me, I am here to remember your great love for me. I am sorry for the times I have not returned your love. May these Stations of the Cross open my heart more and more to the great gift of your love!

The First Station

Jesus Is Condemned to Death

Leader: We adore you, O Christ,
and we bless you.
Response: Because by your holy cross
you have redeemed the world.

Reader: Pilate said to the crowds, "What
should I do with Jesus who is called the
Messiah?" They all shouted, "Crucify
him!" . . . So Pilate released the criminal
Barabbas; and after flogging Jesus, he
handed him over to be crucified.
(See Matthew 27:22, 26)

All: Dear Jesus, your enemies wanted to
kill you, even though you had done
nothing wrong. I pray for those who
suffer unjustly. Have mercy on us.

The Second Station

Jesus Accepts His Cross

Leader: We adore you, O Christ,
and we bless you.

Response: Because by your holy cross
you have redeemed the world.

Reader: After mocking Jesus, the soldiers
stripped him of the robe they had put on
him and put his own clothes back on him.
Then they led Jesus away to crucify him.
(See Matthew 27:31)

All: Dear Jesus, you loved us so much that
you were willing to carry the heavy cross.
Help those who are in pain to remember
that you are always with them. Have
mercy on us.

The Third Station

Jesus Falls the First Time

Leader: We adore you, O Christ,
and we bless you.
Response: Because by your holy cross
you have redeemed the world.

Reader: Jesus bore our sins in his body on
the cross, so that we would be free from
our sins and might live for righteousness;
by Jesus's wounds you have been healed.
(See 1 Peter 2:24)

All: Dear Jesus, it must have been so
painful to fall, and so difficult to get up
after you fell. Help me when it is hard
for me to do the right thing. Have mercy
on us.

The Fourth Station

Jesus Meets His Mother

Leader: We adore you, O Christ,
and we bless you.
Response: Because by your holy cross
you have redeemed the world.

Reader: Simeon blessed Jesus, Mary, and
Joseph and then said to Mary, "Your child
is destined for the fall and the rise of many
in Israel; and he will be a sign that will be
opposed so that the inner thoughts of many
will be revealed—and a sword will pierce
your own soul too." (See Luke 2:34–35)

All: Dear Jesus, your mother, Mary, wanted
to be near you, even though it made her
sad to see you suffer so much. I pray for
those in my family who may be suffering.
Help me to comfort them. Have mercy
on us.

The Fifth Station

Simon of Cyrene Helps Jesus Carry His Cross

Leader: We adore you, O Christ,
and we bless you.
Response: Because by your holy cross
you have redeemed the world.

Reader: As the soldiers led Jesus away, they seized Simon of Cyrene, a man who had come from the countryside, and they laid the cross on him, and made him carry it behind Jesus. (See Luke 23:26)

All: Dear Jesus, Simon helped you at a very difficult time. Help me to use every opportunity I have to be kind to others, because when I am kind, I am helping you carry your cross. Have mercy on us.

The Sixth Station

Veronica Wipes Jesus's Face

Leader: We adore you, O Christ,
and we bless you.
Response: Because by your holy cross
you have redeemed the world.

Reader: Jesus taught the people, "When I
was hungry, you gave me food. When I was
thirsty you gave me something to drink.
When I was a stranger you welcomed me.
When I was naked you gave me clothing
to wear. When I was sick you took care of
me. When I was in prison you visited me.
Whenever you do any of these things for
the least of my brothers and sisters, you
truly did it for me."
(See Matthew 25:35, 40)

All: Dear Jesus, Veronica was courageous
enough to comfort and help you without
worrying what people thought of her. I
pray for all those who give their time to
help others. Have mercy on us.

The Seventh Station

Jesus Falls the Second Time

Leader: We adore you, O Christ,
and we bless you.
Response: Because by your holy cross
you have redeemed the world.

Reader: If God is on our side, who can be against us? God did not even withhold his own Son, but gave him up for all of us. Will God, who gives us Jesus, not also give us everything else? (See Romans 8:31–32)

All: Dear Jesus, when you fell again, you must have wondered if anyone would help you this time. Be with all people who are discouraged and need someone to help them. Have mercy on us.

The Eighth Station

Jesus Speaks to the Women of Jerusalem

Leader: We adore you, O Christ,
and we bless you.
Response: Because by your holy cross
you have redeemed the world.

Reader: A great number of the people
followed Jesus as he walked to Calvary,
and among them were women who were
crying for him with great sorrow. Jesus
turned to them and said, "Daughters of
Jerusalem, don't weep for me, weep for
yourselves and for your children."
(See Luke 23:27–28)

All: Dear Jesus, these women were crying
for you in the middle of a crowd that was
yelling and laughing at you. Help me to
have compassion on those who are sad
and suffering. Have mercy on us.

The Ninth Station

Jesus Falls the Third Time

Leader: We adore you, O Christ,
and we bless you.
Response: Because by your holy cross
you have redeemed the world.

Reader: A person from whom others turn
away and hide their faces; he was a man of
suffering and was acquainted with grief.
He was despised, and we held no respect
for him. He carried both our infirmities
and our diseases; yet we counted him
stricken, struck down by God, and
afflicted. (See Isaiah 53:3–4)

All: Dear Jesus, it must have been almost
impossible for you to get up and keep
going. Free people who are addicted to
alcohol or drugs, who also find it almost
impossible to keep going. Have mercy
on us.

The Tenth Station

Jesus's Clothes Are Torn Off

Leader: We adore you, O Christ,
and we bless you.
Response: Because by your holy cross
you have redeemed the world.

Reader: Is there anyone or anything that
can separate us from the love of Christ?
Can hardship, distress, persecution, famine,
nakedness, danger, or fear of death separate
us from love? ... I am convinced that
nothing ... not anything in all creation can
or will separate us from the love of God in
Christ Jesus our Lord.
(See Romans 8:35, 38–39)

All: Dear Jesus, having your clothes torn
off must have been an embarrassing
and painful moment for you. I pray for
all those who live in poverty and who
are ashamed that they do not have the
clothes and food they need. Have mercy
on us.

The Eleventh Station

Jesus Is Nailed to the Cross

Leader: We adore you, O Christ,
and we bless you.
Response: Because by your holy cross
you have redeemed the world.

Reader: When Jesus and the soldiers arrived at the place that is called The Skull, they crucified Jesus there with two criminals, one on his right and one on his left. Then Jesus said, "Father, forgive them; for they do not know what they are doing."
(See Luke 23:33–34)

All: Dear Jesus, you suffered the pain of being nailed to the cross because you loved us. Be with all the people who feel unloved. Help me to be a loving person. Have mercy on us.

The Twelfth Station

Jesus Dies on the Cross

Leader: We adore you, O Christ,
and we bless you.
Response: Because by your holy cross
you have redeemed the world.

Reader: After hanging on the cross for
a few hours, Jesus gave a loud cry and
breathed his last. When the centurion who
stood facing Jesus saw the way that Jesus
cried out and died, he said, "Truly this man
was God's Son!" (See Mark 15:37–39)

All: Dear Jesus, as you were dying on the
cross, you prayed to your Father and you
thought of each of us with love. I thank
you for dying for me, and I pray for all
those who have died. Have mercy on us.

The Thirteenth Station

Jesus Is Taken Down from the Cross

Leader: We adore you, O Christ,
and we bless you.
Response: Because by your holy cross
you have redeemed the world.

Reader: Joseph from Arimathea, who was
a rich man and also a disciple of Jesus,
came when it was evening. Since Jesus was
already dead, Joseph went to Pilate and
asked for the body of Jesus so that he could
bury him. Pilate ordered that Jesus's body
be given to Joseph. Joseph took the body
and wrapped it in a clean linen cloth.
(See Matthew 27:57–59)

All: Dear Jesus, it was very painful for your
mother and your friends to see you dead.
Comfort those who are mourning
because someone they love has died.
Have mercy on us.

The Fourteenth Station

Jesus Is Laid in the Tomb

Leader: We adore you, O Christ,
and we bless you.
Response: Because by your holy cross
you have redeemed the world.

Reader: Jesus's body was laid in a tomb
carved from rock where no one else had
ever been buried. . . . The women who had
come from Galilee with Jesus followed.
They saw the tomb and how his body was
laid. Then the women left the tomb and
went to prepare spices and ointments with
which to anoint Jesus's body.
(See Luke 23:53–56)

All: Dear Jesus, when you were buried,
your friends were afraid that they would
never see you again. Help all those who
live in fear because of war, fighting, or
terrorism. Let them know that you are
close to them. Have mercy on us.

The Fifteenth Station

Jesus Rises from the Dead

Leader: We adore you, O Christ, and we
bless you.

Response: Because by your holy cross you
have redeemed the world.

Reader: Early at dawn on the first day of
the week, the women came to the tomb,
bringing the spices and ointments that they
had prepared. Instead of finding the tomb
as they had left it on Friday, they saw that
the large stone had been rolled away from
the entrance. When the women went into
the tomb, they did not find the body of
Jesus. . . . They were scared when what
looked like two men dressed in dazzling
clothes suddenly stood beside them. The
women bowed their faces to the ground
and the angels said to them, "Why do you
look for the living among the dead? Jesus is
not here; Jesus is risen." (See Luke 24:1–5)

All: Dear Jesus, you were raised from the dead and you give us new life, too! May all Christians live the new life that we have received in Baptism. Have mercy on us.

Closing Prayer

Dear Jesus, thank you for loving me so much. I want always to remember your great love, and to love you and all my brothers and sisters more and more every day. I want to think, speak, and act as you would; I want you to live in me! Help me to be a messenger of your love, peace, and joy everywhere I go. Amen.

OUR
CATHOLIC
FAITH

Prayer is a vital part of our lives and the life of the Church. The sacraments are also an important part of our life. God has given us the sacraments so that God's grace and life can dwell in us and help us to lead good lives.

THE
SEVEN SACRAMENTS

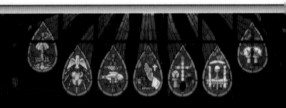

Baptism

Confirmation

Holy Eucharist

Reconciliation (Penance)

Anointing of the Sick

Holy Orders

Matrimony

*All the sacraments have special prayers
associated with them. In this section we will
be looking more closely at the prayers associated
with the sacraments of Holy Eucharist and
Reconciliation.*

Holy Eucharist

The Mass brings the sacrifice of Jesus Christ to us. The Mass is also called the Eucharistic Celebration. It is the high point of our expression of faith as Catholics.

During the Mass we listen to and learn from the Bible through the Liturgy of the Word. In addition, Jesus is made truly present in the consecrated bread and wine, and we receive him in Holy Communion during the Liturgy of the Eucharist.

In building our relationship with God, we are invited to fully participate in the Mass. We do this by singing the songs, listening attentively, and responding appropriately during the whole Mass. To aid you in this, it may be helpful to follow the readings and say the responses as they appear in a missalette.

In the Mass, Jesus offers himself to the heavenly Father for us. We can follow Jesus's example by offering ourselves with Jesus to our heavenly Father. In the Mass, Jesus makes himself our food. We can prepare our hearts to receive Jesus in Holy Communion. After receiving Jesus, we can pray and tell him how much we love him.

Prayer Before Receiving
Holy Communion

Jesus, I believe that you are really present in the Holy Eucharist. You invite me to receive you. I am sorry for the times that I have offended you. Please forgive me. I want to be like you in everything. Take my heart and fill me with your life. Amen.

Prayer After Receiving
Holy Communion

Dear Jesus, you are present in my heart. Thank you for coming to me. Help me to follow you in everything that I think, say, and do. Bless our pope, our bishop, and all who love and follow you. Take care of all the people I love. Comfort those who are sick or lonely. Help all the people in the world to live in peace with you and with each other. I love you and want always to be close to you. Amen.

In addition to receiving Jesus in the Holy Eucharist, we can also adore Jesus in the Blessed Sacrament.

Prayer When Visiting Jesus in the Blessed Sacrament

Jesus, you said, "Come to me, all you who labor and are heavily burdened, and I will give you rest." Today I have come to visit you. You are here for me. When I visit you, I am visiting my best friend. Thank you for your presence and your love.

I believe in your presence, Jesus. I believe that you are looking at me and listening to my prayers. You are so great and so holy; I adore you. You have given me everything; I thank you. I am sorry for the times I have hurt you. Thank you for your mercy.

Jesus, I ask you for the graces that I need. Bless my family, my friends, those who are suffering, and everyone in the world. I believe in you. I hope in you. I love you! I give my whole heart to you. Amen.

Benediction of the Blessed Sacrament

Here are the hymns and prayers that we use at Benediction of the Blessed Sacrament.

O Saving Victim

O Saving Victim, opening wide
The gate of heav'n to us below!
Our foes press on from every side:
Your aid supply, your strength bestow.

To your great name be endless praise,
Immortal Godhead, One in Three;
Oh, grant us endless length of days
In our true native land with thee. Amen.

Humbly Let Us Voice Our Homage

Down in adoration falling
For so great a sacrament:
Let all former rites surrender
To the Lord's New Testament;
What our senses fail to fathom
Let us grasp through faith's consent!

Glory, honor, adoration
Let us sing with one accord!
Praised be God, almighty Father;
Praised be Christ, his Son, our Lord;
Praised be God the Holy Spirit;
Triune Godhead be adored! Amen.

The Divine Praises

Blessed be God.
Blessed be his holy Name.
Blessed be Jesus Christ,
    true God and true man.
Blessed be the Name of Jesus.
Blessed be his most Sacred Heart.
Blessed be his most Precious Blood.
Blessed be Jesus in the most holy
    Sacrament of the altar.
Blessed be the Holy Spirit,
    the Paraclete.
Blessed be the great Mother of God,
    Mary most holy.
Blessed be her holy and Immaculate
    Conception.
Blessed be her glorious assumption.
Blessed be the name of Mary,
    Virgin and Mother.
Blessed be Saint Joseph,
    her most chaste spouse.
Blessed be God in his angels
    and in his saints.

Reconciliation

The sacrament of Reconciliation is one of the most beautiful opportunities to experience God's love and mercy a person can have. In it, we acknowledge our sins, ask God to forgive us, and then receive his healing grace. We thank God for the great gift of this sacrament.

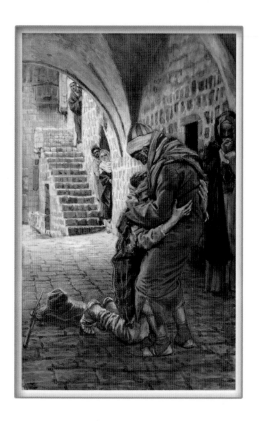

147

Prayer Before Reconciliation

God my Father, you invite me to come closer to you through this sacrament, but some of my choices keep me from the happiness you offer me. Help me to remember any times I may have offended you or hurt other people.

Jesus, I am sorry for the times I did not follow your way. I want to make better choices from now on.

Holy Spirit, fill me with trust as I celebrate the sacrament of Reconciliation. Amen.

After doing the penance given to you by the priest, you can pray this prayer:

Prayer After Reconciliation

God my Father, you have forgiven me! Thank you—help me to be loving and strong.

Jesus, I promise to try to live in a better way from now on.

Holy Spirit, help me to live and grow in your grace. Amen.

How to Go to Confession

In the sacrament of Reconciliation, the priest gives us the forgiveness of God and the Church. To prepare for and receive the sacrament of Reconciliation, follow these six steps:

1. Think of your sins (see page 151 for an examination of conscience).

2. Be sorry for them.

3. Confess (tell) your sins to the priest.

4. Promise Jesus that you will try not to sin again (the Act of Contrition, page 13).

5. Receive God's forgiveness through the prayer of absolution that the priest says.

6. Do or pray the penance the priest gives you.

Examination of Conscience

Jesus, you invite me to look at my choices together with you. Help me to see the ways that you have been present in my life and speaking to me. Help me to see the ways that I have listened to and followed you. Thank you for these times. Help me also to see the times that I have not listened to you, and to be truly sorry for those times. Be with me as I ask myself these questions:

Read the Ten Commandments (pages 152–155). Have I kept these commandments in the way I have lived?

Read the Spiritual and Corporal Works of Mercy (page 156–157). Have I made the most of the opportunities for me to do these actions? Have I lived as a person of mercy?

THE TEN COMMANDMENTS

Jesus, let your commandments guide me in everything I do:

1. I am the Lord your God: You shall not have other gods before me.

I keep God's first commandment by not putting anything else in God's place, and by worshiping and adoring God alone.

2. You shall not take the name of the Lord your God in vain.

I keep God's second commandment by speaking of God, the saints, and holy things with reverence and respect.

3. Remember to keep holy the Lord's day.

I keep God's third commandment by doing my best to attend Mass on Sundays and holy days of obligation. I listen to God's word and, with the priest, offer Jesus to the Father.

4. Honor your father and mother.

I keep God's fourth commandment by loving, respecting, and obeying my parents or guardians, and by paying attention to my teachers and others who have authority over me.

5. You shall not kill.

I keep God's fifth commandment by taking care of my body and soul, and showing the same respect for others. I do not fight or quarrel or hurt anyone, and I try to be kind to everyone.

6. You shall not commit adultery.

I keep God's sixth commandment by being faithful and loyal in my relationships, and by treating my body and others with respect. I only look at TV shows, movies, and things on the Internet that are good for my soul and appropriate for children.

7. You shall not steal.

I keep God's seventh commandment by being honest, refusing to cheat, and not taking or damaging what belongs to others.

8. You shall not bear false witness against your neighbor.

I keep God's eighth commandment by saying only the truth. I do not gossip or tell lies about anyone.

9. You shall not covet your neighbor's wife.

I keep God's ninth commandment by respecting myself and others, and by remembering that our bodies are gifts from God.

10. You shall not covet your neighbor's goods.

I keep God's tenth commandment by being happy with what I have, and trying not to be envious of what belongs to others.

THE SPIRITUAL AND CORPORAL WORKS OF MERCY

Jesus, help me to serve you in these special works of mercy:

The Corporal Works of Mercy

1. To feed those who are hungry

2. To give drink to those who are thirsty

3. To give clothing to those who do not have any

4. To visit those who are in prison

5. To give shelter to those who are homeless

6. To visit those who are sick

7. To bury those who have died

The Spiritual Works of Mercy

1. To instruct others in the faith

2. To give advice to those who are not sure of their faith

3. To comfort those who are sad

4. To be patient

5. To be forgiving

6. To help those who do wrong understand that their action is a sin

7. To pray for all people, living and dead

THE SEASONS
OF THE CHURCH

The Church year is called a liturgical year. The liturgical year begins not on January 1 but with the First Sunday of Advent. We can pray throughout the liturgical year.

Prayer During Advent

During Advent, we prepare our hearts for the coming of Jesus into the world and into our lives. You can pray the Advent prayer each day of Advent.

Come, Lord Jesus! We prepare for your coming into the world and into our hearts. You come to bring God's love to us. The whole world is waiting for this love. People are poor, hungry, hurting, and suffering. We, too, are waiting for your love. Open our hearts and help us to receive you. Come, Lord Jesus, come! Amen.

Prayer During Christmas

During Christmas, we celebrate the birth of Jesus. You can pray the Christmas prayer during the Christmas season, which lasts from Christmas (December 25) until the feast of the Baptism of the Lord (usually the third Sunday after Christmas day).

Jesus, you were born to bring salvation and love to the world. Every time I help someone in need, I celebrate your birth. Every time I smile at someone who is sad, I celebrate your birth. Every time I give someone my love, I celebrate your birth. May I celebrate your birth often and every day! Amen.

Prayer During Lent

During the forty days of Lent, we try to deepen how we live the Gospel of Jesus in order to prepare for his resurrection at Easter. This time of penance and conversion is a gift because it gives us the opportunity to reflect on how we are living, and ask for God's grace to grow in faith. You can pray the Lent prayer from Ash Wednesday through Holy Thursday.

Have mercy on me, God, because you love me. Take away all my sins and give me your grace. I know that I have not always behaved as you would want. Help me, God, to grow closer to you during this Lent. Give me a new heart that is full of love for you. Make me happy by reminding me that you have saved me. Help me to become more like you each day. Amen.

Prayer During Easter

Easter begins with the Easter Vigil Mass—when Jesus rose from the dead—and continues for fifty days until Pentecost—which is when we remember the gift of the Holy Spirit upon Mary and the apostles. During the Easter season, the Church joyfully recalls what Jesus said: "Go out to all the world and tell the good news."

Alleluia! Jesus, you are risen! All of creation, heaven, and the angels rejoice! By rising from the dead, you have given us new life. When you told your disciples to "go out to all the world," you were also telling the same to all who would come to believe. I believe that you are the Son of God, and that you have conquered both sin and death. Give me the grace of your Holy Spirit that I too may tell the people I know about the new life that you give. Let the joy of your resurrection fill all our lives. Alleluia! Amen.

Prayer During Ordinary Time

Ordinary Time is the time when we are not celebrating Advent, Christmas, Lent, or Easter. During Ordinary Time, we hear about Jesus and his ministry, and we are invited to follow him in our everyday lives.

Jesus, you said, "I am the Way, and the Truth, and the Life." I believe that you want to be the Way, the Truth, and the Life for me every day. I believe that you want to show me the way to be holy. I believe that you always spoke the truth. I believe that you give me yourself in Scripture and in your Body and Blood, and that because of you, I have new life. I welcome your truth into my mind, your way into my will, and your life into my heart. Be with me as I go to school, spend time with family and friends, develop my gifts and talents, and learn about you. I offer you my whole life. Amen.

Acknowledgments

Painting by James Tissot. *Jeunesse de Jésus (The Youth of Jesus)*, 1886–1894, https://www.brooklynmuseum.org/opencollection/objects/4446/The_Youth_of_Jesus_Jeunesse_de_J%C3%A9sus. Digital image courtesy of the Brooklyn Museum, purchased by public subscription, vi.

Painting by William-Adolphe Bouguereau. *Compassion*, 1897, http://commons.wikimedia.org/wiki/File:William-Adolphe_Bouguereau_(1825-1905)_-_Compassion_(1897).jpg. Digital image courtesy of Wikimedia Commons, 15.

Painting by William-Adolphe Bouguereau. *L'Innocence*, 1893, http://commons.wikimedia.org/wiki/File:Bouguereau-Linnocence.jpg. Digital image courtesy of Wikimedia Commons, 21.

Painting by William Brassey Hole. *The Wedding at Cana* in "The Life of Jesus of Nazareth: Eighty Pictures" (Eyre & Spottiswoode, 1906), http://commons.wikimedia.org/wiki/File:The_wedding_at_Cana.jpg. Digital image courtesy of Wikimedia Commons, 22.

Painting by James Tissot. *Le magnificat (The Magnificat)*, 1886–1894. http://www.brooklynmuseum.org/opencollection/objects/4425/The_Magnificat_Le_magnificat. Digital image courtesy of the Brooklyn Museum, purchased by public subscription, 29.

Painting by William-Adolphe Bouguereau. *La Vierge à l'agneau (Virgin and Lamb)*, 1903, http://commons.wikimedia.org/wiki/File:William_Adolphe_Bouguereau_Virgin_and_Lamb.jpg. Digital image courtesy of Wikimedia Commons, 30.

Photo by Irena Plahuta. The main altar of Virgin Mary Protectress (jacketed) in the Bazilika Marije Zavetnice in Ptujska Gora, Slovenia, fifteenth century. Adapted from http://commons.wikimedia.org/wiki/File:Ptujska_gora_oltar.JPG. Courtesy of Wikimedia Commons, 36–39.

Tempera on wood by Francesco Botticini. *I tre Arcangeli e Tobias (Three Archangels with Tobias)* c. 1470, http://commons.wikimedia.org/wiki/File:Francesco_Botticini_-_I_tre_Arcangeli_e_Tobias.jpg. Digital image courtesy of the Uffizi Gallery, 45.

Photo of Saint Faustina Kowalska, before 1938, http://commons.wikimedia.org/wiki/File:Faustyna_Kowalska.png. Digital image courtesy of Wikimedia Commons, 46.

Silver bromide print by Carlo Felice Deasti. *Last Photo of John Bosco Living*, 1887, http://commons.wikimedia.org/wiki/File:San_Giovanni_Bosco.jpg. Digital image courtesy of Wikimedia Commons, 47.

Painting by Pierre Le Ber. *La Vénérable Marguerite Bourgeoys*, c. 1700, http://commons.wikimedia.org/wiki/File:Venerable_Mere_Marguerite_Bourgeoys_%28HS85-10-11385%29.jpg. Digital image courtesy of Canada. Patent and Copyright Office, Library and Archives Canada, 48.

Ink on parchment by Guglielmo Giraldi. *Saint Catherine of Bologna*, c. 1469, http://www.getty.edu/art/gettyguide/artObjectDetails?artobj=4117. Digital image courtesy of the Getty's Open Content Program, 51.

Fresco of Saint Sebastian in the Parish Church of Saint Giovanni Battista, Magliano, Tuscany, Italy, fourteenth century, http://commons.wikimedia.org/wiki/File:Fresco_of_Saint_Sebastian_in_Magliano,_Tuscany,_Italy.jpg. Digital image courtesy of the Wikimedia Commons, 52.

Painted panel by Cristoforo Moretti. Genesius, 1451–1475, http://www.museopoldipezzoli.it/en/search.html?field_periodo_value_many_to_one=All&field_collezione_value_many_to_one=All&keys=Saint+Genesius. Digital image courtesy of the Museo Poldi Pezzoli, 54.

Painting by Rafael. *La disputa del sacramento (Disputation of Holy Sacrament)*, 1509–10, http://commons.wikimedia.org/wiki/File:Raphael1a.jpg. Digital image courtesy of Musei Vaticani, 62.

Painting by Anton Dieffenbach. *Rast im Wald (Rest in the Forest)*, before 1914, https://www.van-ham.com/datenbank-archiv/datenbank/anton-dieffenbach/rast-im-wald-1.html. Digital image courtesy of Van Ham Kunstauktionen, 69.

Photo by Evelyn Simak. Stained glass window by Powell of London in the tower of All Saints Church in Alburgh, Norfolk, England, fifteenth century, http://commons.wikimedia.org/wiki/File:All_Saints_church_in_Alburgh_-_stained_glass_window_-_geograph.org.uk_-_1770510.jpg. Courtesy of Wikimedia Commons, 71.

Painting by James Tissot. *La fille de Zäire (The Daughter of Jairus)*, 1886–1896, https://www.brooklynmuseum.org/opencollection/objects/4496/The_Daughter_of_Jairus_La_fille_de_Z%C3%A4ire. Digital image courtesy of the Brooklyn Museum, purchased by public subscription, 83.

Painting by Thomas Cole. *The Pilgrim of the Cross at the End of His Journey*, 1846–1848, http://americanart.si.edu/collections/search/artwork/?id=5078. Digital image courtesy of the Smithsonian American Art Museum, 84.

Detail of sculpture by Francesco Nagni, twentieth century. Photo courtesy of the Daughters of St. Paul, 85.

Painting by James Tissot. *Il les envoya deux à deux (He Sent Them Out Two by Two)*, 1886–1896, https://www.brooklynmuseum.org/opencollection/objects/4517/He_Sent_them_out_Two_by_Two_Il_les_envoya_deux_%C3%A0_deux. Digital image courtesy of the Brooklyn Museum, purchased by public subscription, 87.

Painting by James Tissot. *Notre-Seigneur Jésus-Christ (Our Lord Jesus Christ)*, 1886–1894, https://www.brooklynmuseum.org/opencollection/objects/4553/Our_Lord_Jesus_Christ_Notre-Seigneur_J%C3%A9sus-Christ. Digital image courtesy of the Brooklyn Museum, purchased by public subscription, 139.

Engraving by Gustave Doré. *Heavenly host singing Gloria in Excelsis in The Vision of Purgatory and Paradise; TOGETHER WITH: The Vision of Hell.* Two vols. Translated by H.F. Cary, and Illustrated with the designs of Gustave Dore. With Critical and Explanatory Notes, Life of Dante, and Chronology. (London and New York: Cassell, Petter, and Galpin, c. 1880), http://commons.wikimedia.org/wiki/File:Par_27.jpg. Digital image courtesy of Wikimedia Commons, 145.

Painting by James Tissot. *Le retour de l'enfant prodigue (The Return of the Prodigal Son)*, 1886–1894, https://www.brooklynmuseum.org/opencollection/objects/4538/The_Return_of_the_Prodigal_Son_Le_retour_de_lenfant_prodigue. Digital image courtesy of the Brooklyn Museum, purchased by public subscription, 147.

Photo by Reinhardhauke, Rosette window in Jouarre Abbey of Notre Dame Cathedral, France, fourteenth century. Adapted from http://commons.wikimedia.org/wiki/File: Abbaye—Notre-Dame_de_Jouarre6927.jpg. Digital image courtesy of Wikimedia Commons, cover.

BOOKS & MEDIA

The Daughters of St. Paul operate book and media centers at the following addresses. Visit, call, or write the one nearest you today, or find us at www.pauline.org.

CALIFORNIA
3908 Sepulveda Blvd, Culver City, CA 90230   310-397-8676
935 Brewster Avenue, Redwood City, CA 94063   650-369-4230
5945 Balboa Avenue, San Diego, CA 92111   858-565-9181

FLORIDA
145 S.W. 107th Avenue, Miami, FL 33174   305-559-6715

HAWAII
1143 Bishop Street, Honolulu, HI 96813   808-521-2731

ILLINOIS
172 North Michigan Avenue, Chicago, IL 60601   312-346-4228

LOUISIANA
4403 Veterans Memorial Blvd, Metairie, LA 70006   504-887-7631

MASSACHUSETTS
885 Providence Hwy, Dedham, MA 02026   781-326-5385

MISSOURI
9804 Watson Road, St. Louis, MO 63126   314-965-3512

NEW YORK
64 West 38th Street, New York, NY 10018   212-754-1110

SOUTH CAROLINA
243 King Street, Charleston, SC 29401   843-577-0175

TEXAS
Currently no book center; for parish exhibits or outreach evangelization, contact: 210-569-0500, or SanAntonio@paulinemedia.com, or P.O. Box 761416, San Antonio, TX 78245

VIRGINIA
1025 King Street, Alexandria, VA 22314   703-549-3806

CANADA
3022 Dufferin Street, Toronto, ON M6B 3T5   416-781-9131